D1330052

TABLE OF CONTENTS

CHAPTER 1:

Behind The Shadow

*Corruption is worse than prostitution. The latter might
endanger the morals of an individual; the former
invariably endangers the morals of the entire country.*
- Karl Kraus

A shadow government (cryptocracy, secret government, or invisible government) is a group of conspiracy theories based on the notion that real and actual political power resides not with publicly elected representatives but with private Individuals who are exercising power behind the scenes, beyond the scrutiny of democratic institutions. According to this belief, the official elected government is subservient to the shadow government, which is the true executive power. Some of the groups proposed by these theories as constituting the shadow government include central banks; Freemasons, intelligence agencies; think tanks; organized Jewry; the Vatican; secret societies; Jesuits; moneyed interests; globalist elites and supranational organizations who seek to manipulate policy in their own interest or in order to serve a larger agenda that is hidden from the general public.

The mainstream media's agenda is clear. They want you to believe

1

that conspiracies don't exist, the world is exactly like they say it is, and anyone who disagrees is to be marginalized, mocked and shamed.

Behind the shadows is this deep state which is a combination of elected and appointed members of the legislative and executive branches, and corporate insiders, especially the military-industrial complex, Wall Street, and Silicon Valley. Together, fueled by enormous amounts of money, they effectively control the country, regardless of which party is in power or the wishes of the electorate.

The Manhattan Project

Government Insider Lofgren believes the '*deep state*' in its current form began with the Manhattan Project during WW II. This is where a series of events started taking place that really began to frame the climate we are in now.

At the start of World War II, the United States had no civilian agency dedicated to gathering foreign intelligence. Not that Americans never spied: The Army and Navy both had intelligence branches, and even private companies like General Electric sponsored corporate espionage. But the genteel Ivy Leaguers who ruled the federal government tended to view such activity as immoral, even dirty. As President Franklin D. Roosevelt's

2

secretary of war, Henry Stimson, once said, *"Gentlemen don't read each other's mail."* This squeamishness put the United States at a disadvantage compared with Great Britain, Germany, and Russia, all of which had sophisticated intelligence bureaus and happily spied on adversaries and allies alike.

Pearl Harbor finally forced the U.S. government to admit its shortcomings and establish the Office of Strategic Services. Most people know it today as the precursor to the Central Intelligence Agency, but OSS's primary mandate was broader than that. In addition to espionage, it carried out paramilitary operations overseas and helped pave the way for the U.S. military's Special Forces. In many cases, the espionage and the extralegal activities went hand in hand.

OSS was primarily shaped by two men: its director, William *"Wild Bill"* Donovan, and its chief scientist, Stanley Lovell. Donovan first won fame during World War I for leading a spectacularly idiotic assault. He commanded the 69th Infantry of New York, the famous *"Fighting Irish,"* who were trying to conquer a German fortress in the Argonne Forest in October 1918. During an intense shoot-out one day, Donovan received orders to fall back. After considering his options, he ordered his men to charge instead. When the Fighting Irish hesitated, he screamed, "What's the matter with you? You want to live forever?" and charged off alone, confident his men would follow. They did.

The Germans stopped them cold, and a machine-gun bullet shattered Donovan's knee. But he once again refused orders to evacuate and spent the next five hours hobbling around and preparing his men for the inevitable German counterassault. When it came, he rallied the Fighting Irish and drove the Huns back into the fortress in a rout, all but winning the battle single-handedly. Had the assault failed, Donovan would have been court-martialed (assuming he even lived). As it was, he earned the Medal of Honor and returned home one of the most highly decorated soldiers in American history.

When World War II rolled around, Donovan was working in a New York law firm. He happened to have attended law school at Columbia with Franklin D. Roosevelt, and Roosevelt sent his old chum to England in July 1940 to provide a more accurate picture of events there than Joseph Kennedy Sr., the defeatist ambassador to the U.K., could. Although Donovan agreed that things were grim, he emphasized the grit of the British people and singled out Winston Churchill—who wasn't even prime minster yet—as a stupendous leader. The assessment bucked up FDR's spirits and contributed to the Churchill-Roosevelt alliance that would ultimately help defeat Hitler.

Donovan parlayed his field trip to England into a job as Roosevelt's coordinator of intelligence, and from there he founded OSS and became its chief. But while the role made sense on paper—Donovan clearly had the vision and drive to see OSS succeed—Wild Bill also lacked pretty much every other skill necessary to run a government agency. Even those who adored him admitted that he had "*abysmal*" if not "*atrocious*"

administrative skills, and he simply didn't have the patience or fortitude to manage people. As a result, OSS became one of the most poorly run agencies in American history. Employees used to laugh over a line from Macbeth that perfectly summed up the enterprise: *"Confusion now has made his masterpiece."*

Nowhere were Donovan's flaws more evident than in his hiring practices. Needing to throw together an agency quickly, he turned to his circle of friends in New York and hired 'blue bloods' by the dozen. The OSS roster was lousy with Mellons, Du Ponts, Morgans, and Vanderbilts. Columnists joked that the agency's initials actually stood for *"Oh So Social."* In Donovan's defense, hiring aristocrats did make sense on some level: They usually spoke several languages and knew Europe well. But holidays on the Riviera were a far cry from war. As one reporter noted, "Knowing how to speak French in a tux didn't necessarily prepare recruits for parachuting into enemy territory or blowing up bridges." More than a few heirs and heiresses suffered "dramatic mental crackups" in the field.

Even more than aristocrats, however, Donovan loved misfits, and he staffed OSS with a bizarre array of talent. There were mafia contract killers and theology professors. There were bartenders, anthropologists, and pro wrestlers. There were orthodontists, ornithologists, and felons on leave from federal penitentiaries. Marlene Dietrich, Julia Child, John Steinbeck, John Wayne, Leo Tolstoy's grandson, and a Ringling circus heir all pitched in as well. Observers sometimes referred to OSS as *"St. Elizabeths,"* after the well-known Washington, D.C., lunatic asylum. One top official there admitted that *"OSS may indeed have employed quite a few psychopathic characters."* Donovan once said, *"I'd*

put Stalin on the OSS payroll if I thought it would help defeat Hitler." No one knew whether he was kidding.

This was the start of the growing world of intelligence agencies playing fast and loose around the planet, a secret government lodged inside the one they knew that even the president didn't fully control.

JFK – sudden agenda changes, back channels

Although Kennedy was elected in 1960 as a Cold Warrior, he moved away from a hardline stance almost immediately after being elected. In 1961, he refused to provide U.S. military support to the CIA's bungling Bay of Pigs invasion of Cuba, something that many in the CIA never forgave him for.

In 1962, during the Cuban Missile Crisis, Kennedy negotiated peace with Russian leader Nikita Khrushchev. This was against much of the advice coming from the deep state, who estimated that, although the United States would lose 80% of its population in a thermonuclear war, the Russians would lose 100% of theirs. So, we would "*win.*" Kennedy rightfully recognized this as sheer insanity.

At the same time that JFK was talking to Khrushchev, CIA agent Bill Harvey was ordering raids on Cuba, in direct violation of Presidential directive, with the goal of provoking a missile launch by the Russians so as to start a war. When the crisis ended, Robert Kennedy had Harvey transferred out of the Western hemisphere so that

he couldn't cause any more such trouble. Harvey never forgave the Kennedy brothers and retained a bitter hatred of them for the rest of his life.

In 1963, just months before his death, President Kennedy gave a historic speech at American University, outlining a vision for peaceful coexistence between the United States and Russia. It featured prominently in Oliver Stone's film JFK, which is worth watching in its entirety.

Kennedy negotiated a peace with the Russians during the missile crisis, and at the time of his death, he was making overtures to Fidel Castro, as well as beginning to withdraw U.S. troops from Vietnam. Historians disagree about whether Kennedy was serious about peace with Cuba, as there were also plans for an all-out invasion of the island happening at the same time. But regarding Vietnam, more and more support for the notion that JFK would not have escalated the conflict has emerged since this thesis was first developed by Peter Dale Scott in the 1970s and then more extensively by John Newman in his 1992 book JFK and Vietnam.

Kennedy was a user of "back channels" for sensitive communications. In negotiating with the Soviets, messages were passed back and forth between *"Soviet Ambassador Anatoly Dobrynin or other Soviet officials to other members of President Kennedy's official family."* The overtures to Cuba were made through journalist Lisa Howard, and through Ambassador William Attwood. Historian Michael Beschloss, in an

7

article on the back-channel talks in the New York Times, writes that *"Attorney General Robert F. Kennedy worried that such talks would leak and embarrass his brother on the eve of his 1964 re-election campaign, but the president quietly encouraged Attwood to pursue the matter."* The leaks of General Flynn's communications with the Russians and their consequences show that RFK's worries were well-founded.

Meanwhile, as JFK was using back channels to negotiate peace with the Russians and possibly with the Cubans as well, Lyndon Johnson had his own back-channel – to the deep state. This is documented by John Newman in his book, which has just been re-released in a second edition. Generals from the Joint Chiefs of Staff bypassed the President and communicated with the Vice-President instead, who was much more of a hawk on Vietnam than Kennedy was. It took Lyndon Johnson all of two days to reverse Kennedy's plans to withdraw from Vietnam. He is alleged to have said to the Joint Chiefs, *"Just get me elected, and I'll give you your damn war."*

We have heard a few solid theories... It's to be known that supposedly Kennedy was fed up with the shenanigans that the CIA was pulling. He found out the CIA was trying to kill (Cuban leader Fidel) Castro, which is a fact. So, the argument is that the CIA felt that Kennedy was going to disband them. And as a result of that, they were the ones that ordered the killing of Kennedy. As you may know, a former head of the CIA, Allen Dulles, was a member of the Warren Commission, the special Johnson-appointed panel tasked with the official investigation of the assassination. The commission determined that Oswald acted alone.

Oswald was a supporter of Soviet-backed Cuba.
What we know of Oswald was that he was in the Russian embassy in Mexico City. We even know who he talked to. But we don't know what was said. Then a few weeks later, he shoots Kennedy. It may have been something that they overheard involving him and the Russians. Or, maybe the CIA had Oswald on the payroll. He might have been a double agent.

Is it possible that Russians ordered Oswald to do it? Not likely. The Russians would never have ordered Oswald to kill Kennedy because of his well-known links to Russia and his pro-Cuban sympathies. Russia's leaders knew they would have been the first suspects if they'd engineered an assassination by Oswald. It would have been an act of war, which could have triggered a nuclear attack.

Operation Mockingbird – The evidence of the deep state's influence over the media

The CIA spied on and controlled, the American media. CIA project Operation Mockingbird spied on members of the Washington press corps in 1963, 1972 and 1973. They also paid journalists to publish CIA propaganda, wiretapped their phones, and monitored their offices to keep tabs on their activities and visitors.

It was an alleged large-scale project undertaken by the CIA beginning in the 1950s in which they recruited American journalists into a propaganda network. The recruited journalists were put on payroll by the CIA and instructed to write fake stories that promoted the views of the intelligence agency. Student cultural organizations and magazines were allegedly funded as fronts for this operation.

Operation Mockingbird expanded later on in order to influence foreign media as well.

Frank Wisner, the director of the espionage and counter-intelligence branch, spearheaded the organization and was told to concentrate on *"propaganda, economic warfare; preventive direct action, including sabotage, anti-sabotage, demolition and evacuation measures; subversion against hostile states, including assistance to underground resistance groups, and support of indigenous anti-Communist elements in threatened countries of the free world."*

Journalists were reportedly blackmailed and threatened into this network. The CIA's financing of independent and private organizations wasn't just meant to create favorable stories. It was also a means to covertly collect information from other countries that were relevant to America's national security.

Like the New York Times article, Ramparts Magazine exposed the covert operation in 1967 when it reported that the National Student Association received funding from the CIA.

A 1977 article in Rolling Stone, written by Carl Bernstein, was titled *"The CIA and the Media."* Bernstein said in the article that the CIA *"has secretly bankrolled numerous foreign press services, periodicals and newspapers — both English and foreign language — which provided excellent cover for CIA operatives."* These reports led to a series of congressional investigations done in the 1970s under a committee that was set up by the U.S. Senate and named the Church Committee. The Church Committee investigations looked into government operations and potential abuses by the CIA, the NSA, the FBI, and the IRS.

In 2007, around 700 pages of documents from the 1970s were declassified and released by the CIA in a collection called "The Family Jewels." The files all surrounded the investigations and scandals pertaining to agency misconduct during the 1970s.

There was only one mention of Operation Mockingbird in these files, in which it was revealed that two American journalists were wire-tapped for several months.

Though declassified documents show that this type of operation occurred, it's never been officially confirmed as the title of Operation Mockingbird. Thus, it's also never been officially discontinued.

Meddling and more meddling – the *"Global*

deep state"

The U.S. tried to change other countries' governments 72 times during the Cold War...

The CIA has concluded with *"high confidence"* that Russia intervened covertly during the presidential election to promote Donald Trump's candidacy. They based this assessment on the discovery that Russian security agencies had hacked the Republican National Committee, the Democratic National Committee, and the Hillary Clinton campaign —

and had released selected Democratic documents to WikiLeaks to undermine Clinton's candidacy.

If true, Russia's actions are reminiscent of Cold War covert political warfare, with an Internet-era twist. Here are six key things we've uncovered about those efforts.

Between 1947 and 1989, the United States tried to change other nations' governments 72 times! That's a remarkable number. It includes 66 covert operations and six overt ones.

Of course, that doesn't excuse Russia's apparent meddling in the 2016 U.S. presidential election. These 72 U.S. operations took place during the Cold War — meaning that, in most cases, the Soviet Union was covertly supporting anti-U.S. forces on the other side. However, a look at these U.S. actions allows us to survey the covert activities of a major power, so we can glean insight into such interventions' causes and consequences.

Most covert efforts to replace another country's government failed. During the Cold War, for instance, 26 of the United States' covert operations successfully brought a U.S.-backed government to power; the remaining 40 failed. Success depended in large part on the choice of covert tactics. Not a single U.S.-backed assassination plot during this time actually resulted in killing the intended target, although two foreign leaders — South Vietnam's Ngo Dinh Diem and the Dominican Republic's Rafael Trujillo — were killed by foreign intermediaries without Washington's blessing during U.S.-backed coups.

Similarly, covert actions to support militant groups trying to topple a foreign regime nearly always failed. Of 36 attempts, only five overthrew their targets. Sponsoring coups was more successful: nine out of 14 attempted coups put the U.S.-backed leaders in power.

Meddling in foreign elections is the most successful covert tactic (as Russia may not be surprised to learn). We found 16 cases in which Washington sought to influence foreign elections by covertly funding, advising and spreading propaganda for its preferred candidates, often doing so beyond a single election cycle. Of these, the U.S.-backed parties won their elections 75 percent of the time.

Of course, it is impossible to say whether the U.S.-supported candidates would have won their elections without the covert assistance; many were leading in the polls before the U.S. intervention. However, as the CIA's head of the Directorate of Intelligence, Ray S. Cline once put it, the key to a successful covert regime change is

13

"supplying just the right bit of marginal assistance in the right way at the right time."

Regime changes rarely work out as the intervening states expect.

A Trump presidency might not be as much of a boon for Russia as hoped or feared. Clinton warned in the third presidential debate that Putin *"would rather have a puppet as president of the United States."*

However, as shown in a recent International Security article with Alexander Downes, leaders installed via regime change generally don't act as puppets for long. Once in power, the new leaders find that acting at their foreign backers' behest brings significant domestic opposition. They, therefore, tend to moderate their policies or turn against the foreign backer completely. In fact, there are already reports that the Kremlin is feeling *"buyer's remorse"* over Trump's victory, given his unpredictability.

Covert regime change can devastate the target countries
The research found that after a nation's government was toppled, it was less democratic and more likely to suffer civil war, domestic instability, and mass killing. At the very least, citizens lost faith in their governments.

Even if Russia didn't make the difference in electing Trump, it successfully undermined confidence in U.S. political institutions and news media.

The best antidote to subterfuge is transparency
States intervene covertly so that they don't have to be held accountable for their actions. Amid reports that Russian hackers have been emboldened by the success of the DNC hack, exposing Moscow's hand is the first step toward deterring future attacks against the United States and upcoming elections in Germany, France and the Netherlands. It may also be the best way to dispel misinformation and restore faith in U.S. democratic institutions at a time when 55 percent of Americans say they are troubled by Russian interference into the election.

The United States is beginning this effort. Congress has announced bipartisan investigations and Obama ordered a comprehensive report on covert foreign interference into U.S. presidential elections going back to the 2008 election.

The 9/11 War for Oil

The sudden, dramatic drop in oil prices has changed the world almost overnight. Russia's facing an economic crisis, and U.S. consumers are saving a fortune at the pump. The reasons for the sudden swing are not particularly glamorous. They involve factors like supply and demand, oil companies having invested heavily in exploration several years ago to produce a glut of oil that has now hit the market -- and then, perhaps, the *"lack of cohesion"* among the diverse members

of OPEC.

But now, right on cue, out come the conspiracy theorists — including Vladimir Putin — to tell us what's really going on.

Recently, Putin floated the idea that the oil price drop is the result of a U.S.-Saudi plot to hurt his country. *"We all see the lowering of the oil price. There's lots of talk about what's causing it,"* Putin said recently. *"Could it be the agreement between the U.S. and Saudi Arabia to punish Iran and affect the economies of Russia and Venezuela? It could."*

CHAPTER 2:

What is the Deep State?

I f you've merely glanced at a newspaper within the past three years, you've likely seen the term *"deep state."* The complex phrase has emerged into the national conversation in recent years, but the idea has been bubbling up underground far longer than the Trump Presidency.

The belief in a deep state rides party lines, so the definition varies depending on which side of the aisle you stand. According to Time Magazine[1], many conservatives consider the deep state to be, *"the force behind the 'covert resistance' to the President."*

Simply put the entire *"Democratic"* system that exists within the United States today is a sham. It's a mere sideshow that most Americans believe actually means something. Your vote is meaningless for one important reason - the person you vote for is powerless to do anything meaningful, utterly incapable

of effecting any significant change. It doesn't matter whether you vote Republican or Democrat; your candidate will not be able to change a thing.

What I'm saying is that no matter if you vote Republican or Democrat is utterly irrelevant because...the person who's elected can't change anything significantly, because the deep state won't let them.

In the US, *"deep state"* describes a hidden government within the elected government and many theorists believe that this shadow government comprises partly elected officials, partly industry leaders, and largely public service employees – all united under a secret agenda. While originally used to represent the dual government in Turkey, as well as similar establishments in Egypt, Israel, Spain and Italy, it has come to represent a U.S. conspiracy after the infamous WikiLeaks case. The leaker in this case, Edward Snowden, noted: *"the deep state is not just the intelligence agencies, it is really a way of referring to the career bureaucracy of government. These are officials who*

18

sit in powerful positions, who don't leave when presidents do, who watch presidents come and go ... they influence policy, they influence presidents."

Professor Jason Royce Lindsey argues that the deep state draws power from the national security and intelligence communities and Alfred W. McCoy notes that after the 9/11 attacks, the U.S. intelligence community *"has built a fourth branch of the U.S. government"* that is *"in many ways autonomous from the executive, and increasingly so."*

[1]https://time.com/4692178/donald-trump-deep-state-breitbart-barack-obama/

Right-wing media organization Breitbart[2], has gone so far as to claim most operators in the deep state are, *"holdovers from the Obama administration, Republican appointees who disagree with Trump's agenda, as well as several of the 2.8 million career government employees."*

Back in July of 2017, Obama's CIA director John Brennan said at a conference that executive branch officials have an obligation to refuse to carry out anti-democratic orders from President Trump. Rush Limbaugh quickly picked up the comment responding, *"He*

practically called for coop!" a few days later. What Limbo was warning about was some sort of a possible plot orchestrated by embeds in the deep state at Pentagon, State Department and various intelligence agencies.

The deep state became really popular term back in 2017 and came to represent something that operates independently of elected officials. Policy experts have been using the term deep state for years to describe people and organizations who exercise power independent (sometimes over) the elected political leaders. While the term mostly implied the deep state powers in developing countries like Egypt and Turkey, it has recently become a hot topic in the US. The events of 9/11 created the need for surveillance and resulted in growth of an intelligence machine that was typically not accountable to the legal system. Even university professors have begun to describe a dual state system in the United States.

A memo from a National Security Council staffer was published in August 2017 in Foreign Policy. In this memo, the staffer notes that President Trump is being attacked because he represents an *"existential threat to cultural Marxist memes that dominate the prevailing cultural narrative."* It went on to say that Trump threatens the machine that includes *"deep state actors, globalists, bankers, Islamists, and establishment Republicans."* The full memo is seven pages long and titled *"May 2017 – POTUS and the*

Political Warfare." You can read it right here: https://foreignpolicy. com/2017/08/10/heres-the-memo-that-blew-up-the-nsc/

In comparison, many liberals consider the deep state to be nothing more than a conspiracy theory. Amy Zegart, who serves as the co-director of the Center for International Security and Cooperation at Stanford University, was quoted in the New York Times saying, *"it looks and feels like a political witch hunt."* She continued to say the President Trump pushes this deep state rhetoric when people don't agree with him. *"[He] jumps to the conclusion that it must be politicized," Zegart said, "and must be the result of people conspiring against him."*

While politics tend to drive the conversation behind the deep state, to fully comprehend the concept, it is best to understand a non-partisan definition. The New York Times described the deep state as *"a political conflict between a nation's leader and its governing institutions."*

[2]https://www.breitbart.com

Although this has made recent news, this has a deep rooted history and in 1961, outgoing president Dwight D. Eisenhower warned of the influence of the military-industrial complex, a sort of working partnership between the US military and the huge defense industry, constructed chiefly during the two world wars, that supplied and equipped it. Eisenhower saw the two together as a grave risk to American democracy and issued a warning in stark and powerful language.

"In the councils of government, we must guard against the acquisition of unwarranted influence, whether sought or

unsought, by the military–industrial complex. The potential for the disastrous rise of misplaced power exists and will persist. We must never let the weight of this combination endanger our liberties or democratic processes."

The idea of the deep state grew since then…

• In the Bush-Cheney era, the left wing saw the deep state as a conspiracy of military, CIA officials and defense contractors.

• In the Obama era, the concept of the deep state was promoted by Snowden after he leaked tons of classified files to expose government surveillance activities.

• In the Trump era, the deep state became a pronounced issue. Trump's famous plans to "drain the swamp" stirred and upset a lot of people who got very, very comfortable where they were at. Coupled with policy and budget shifts, these plans started a *"war."* It is a bureaucratic turf war where the deep state is fighting to "stay put" amidst Trumps budget cuts. To do that, they had to shift public's attention to Trump – and Trump's attention to having to defend himself. They did it by leaking his supposed conversations with foreign leaders, by attacking him directly from the National Parks Service Twitter account and by turning assumptions into some very dramatic *"outbursts"*, like when the EPA contacted the media *"fearing"* that their latest climate change report will be ignored.

Several analysts and authors on the subject have linked the term deep state to the influence of the military-industrial complex. Author and retired congressional staffer Mike Lofgren has claimed that the *"private"* part of the deep state is made up of the military-industrial complex. In an interview with Truthout.com, Lofgren went so far as to claim that the so-called deep state is *"a hybrid association of elements of government and parts of top-level finance and industry effectively able to govern the US without reference to the consent of the governed."*

In his September 2019 Fox News Article, Jason Chaffetz, a former Utah representative and former Chairman of the U.S. House Oversight Committee - now a Fox News Contributor - describes the deep state as *"a bureaucracy that allowed agencies to become weaponized in the service of political battles."* He goes on to say that in the beginning *"that meant protecting President Obama by using federal power to target political opponents or by covering the tracks of the corrupt or incompetent within his administration. By the time I left Congress, the deep state's focus had shifted to thwarting the administration of the newly elected President Donald Trump."*

Chaffetz goes on to explain the mechanisms the deep state uses to control the status quo:

"Spying is just one trick up the sleeves of politicized bureaucrats. Powerful senior staffers with authority to classify, resist disclosure, and subvert oversight have perfected other strategies to avoid transparency and accountability.

The deep state manipulates congressional investigations by pretending to cooperate with document subpoenas. Those who are part of the deep state bury congressional committees in piles of paper ostensibly responsive to the investigation, and then brag to the media about the number of pages they have turned over. In reality, many of those pages will either be fully redacted, duplicates of other pages, or irrelevant to the investigation. Misleading the public about the nature of documents sought either by Congress or through Freedom of Information Act (FOIA) requests is another art the deep state has perfected. Agencies employ lawyers specifically to find reasons to withhold documents."

In his conversation with Fox News' Sean Hannity, North Carolina Representative Mark Meadows argued that the Russia collusion was a hoax aimed at taking Trump down:

"We talk about the deep state. There are players now, even ambassadors that are sitting ambassadors that were involved in part of this with the FBI and DOJ. So as we look at this, it's time we show the American people what's out there. Declassify some of those documents. I think when the American people have seen what I've seen they will judge for themselves and know that this has all been a hoax."

But the deep state mindset can also infect the elected leaders of the Executive Branch, the President and Vice-President. The so-called Unitary Executive Theory of the Constitution holds that Article 2, which grants the President *"executive power,"* means that no one - not Congress or the courts - can tell the President what do or how to do it, particularly in matters of national security and foreign affairs, where the

24

constitutional authority of other branches is minimal.

Many believe that Vice President Dick Cheney, in poor health and happily *"retired"* as the wealthy CEO of Halliburton, jumped back into government in 2000 when George W. Bush inadvertently presented him with an opportunity to take advantage of the theory by making Cheney his running mate.

Presumably, Cheney exploited Bush's relatively dis-engaged attitude by accepting the Vice Presidency on the condition that he be granted direct authority over energy and foreign affairs. Despite no constitutional language permitting this delegation of power, Bush acquiesced, and Cheney defended the action by referring skeptics to the Unitary Executive Theory.

Since then, the theory has worked its way into several Presidential actions, such as executive orders and the Continuity of Government.

Continuity of Government (COG) – another variation of the deep state

Continuity of Government, or 'COG,' is a simple concept with a complex history. In times of devastating national emergency causing widespread chaos and destruction – such as nuclear war – COG is a step-by-step guide for harried, confused, or even frightened and injured executive branch employees for keeping essential functions of government going.

It is also much more than that. COG requires extensive infrastructure, such as hardened remote bunkers, food supplies and communication channels as well as emergency processes to handle delicate issues such as constitutional succession when executive branch leaders may be dead, missing or unreachable. COG procedures even assure people can prove they are who they say they are - by assigning secret code words to the Vice President and Speaker of the House, for example. It requires extensive planning and huge expenditures, all of it mainly and necessarily secret.

The first COG action dates to late 1776, just months after the Declaration of Independence and years before the Constitution, when British forces advanced on Philadelphia, where the Continental Congress sat. The Congress resolved, if necessary, to dissolve itself and officially reconstitute in Baltimore at a date to be determined. In the event, that is precisely what happened.

In 1952, President Harry Truman ordered COG plans for all executive functions and Congress, which led to construction of secret facilities – many of which are presumably classified to this day. The most widely known is the emergency congressional facility in Greenbrier County, West Virginia.

Presidents Jimmy Carter and Ronald Reagan updated and expanded Truman's original order in the form of Presidential Directives. The result was a what many consider an extra-constitutional executive branch plan whereby if disaster struck, three emergency teams would disperse to separate

26

locations in the American interior, each with its own 'president' and people charged with operating the federal departments. If one 'team' was killed, the next 'team' would take over.

The Directives do not contemplate for how long such teams would operate. Though it can be assumed that three teams would be headed by the President, Vice President and Speaker of the House - the three people constitutionally in line to operate the executive branch - the Directives do not memorialize this. Presumably, as long as the President lived, his or her team would be operating the executive branch, but the Directives are silent as to how the three teams communicate with each other to ascertain the surviving members of each and/or allow the President (or Vice President or Speaker) to avail themselves of the advice of the other teams - presuming some of lead team had not survived.

Under Reagan's Directive, the implementation of COG was expanded beyond nuclear war to include *"natural disaster, military attack, technological emergency, or other emergency, that seriously degrades or seriously threatens the national security of the United States"*.

COG plans have been practiced several times. Richard Clarke, the anti-terror coordinator under Presidents Clinton and George W. Bush, vividly recalls being given short notice to get to Andrews AFB and board a plane that flew a COG team to a desert location (Clarke says to this day he does not know where he was), where the team 'acted out' its roles over a one-week period. Role-playing included details such as not going outside (*"because of the radioactivity"*) to not being allowed to use the phones (*"because they were not connected to anything."*)

27

The COG Directive has been implemented only once - in the immediate aftermath of the 9/11 attacks when the scope and strategic aim of the attacks was uncertain. President Bush, who was in Florida at the time, was flown to Barksdale AFB in Louisiana under fighter escort and then to Offut AFB in Oklahoma before returning to Andrews AFB in Washington. It is not known if his movements were part of the COG plans.

At the White House, President Bush's personal secretary recalls seeing Secret Service agents who, having swept Vice President Dick Cheney literally off his feet, carried him down a hallway after the second plane hit the Word Trade Center.

Cheney, who had been in touch with President Bush and House Speaker Dennis Hastert following the first impact on the WTC, recalls his Secret Service agents entering his office *"saying, 'Sir, we have to leave immediately,' and grabbed me... and they hoisted me up and moved me very rapidly down the hallway, down some stairs, through some doors, and down some more stairs into an underground facility under the White House."*

It was clear that by early afternoon, evacuating the Executive branch would not be necessary.

Well or poorly planned, effective or a bumbling mess, it is no secret that the executive and legislative branches of our government have complex, highly secret, expensive and possibly constitutionally questionable plans to maintain operations in the event of national disaster. The people who may become Presidents or Vice Presidents as part of multiple *"Executive Teams"* may not necessarily be elected officials at all. The general public may be clueless as to who their President may be and it may be that it's not someone who we vote for. People with money and power may easily buy these contingency leadership positions and make decisions that affect national security, economy and more without any consent from the public and will likely lack any expertise when it comes to running a country.

Who does the deep state comprise?

The deep state has a very broad infrastructure, with people of all different levels involved in its operations. Sometimes, they don't even realize they are a part of the machine...

Key parts of the deep state are:

CIA
NSA
FBI
EPA
Department of Agriculture
Department of Commerce
Department of Defense
Department of Education
Department of Energy
Department of Health and Human Services
Department of Homeland Security
Department of Housing and Urban Development (HUD)
Private energy companies with government contracts
Private security companies with government contracts
Private tech companies with government contracts

And many more...

How Can An Average American Such As You Possibly Stand Up to All This Power and Stop The deep state's Takeover Of Our American Liberties?

By gaining the knowledge and the power to stand up against the cancer eating away at our great country. **As a single person you are weak, but as a population over 323 million - strong there is nothing that can stop us, if we have the knowledge and a plan to follow to take action.** That's exactly what we offer in Chapter 5: Taking Action.

CHAPTER 3:

An Abundance of Information

While the deep state has appeared in the form of coups and overthrows in other countries, the deep state in the United States has become synonymous with government leaks.

In 2017, the Committee on Homeland Security and Governmental Affairs, then chaired by Republican Senator Ron Johnson, released a report titled State Secrets: *How an Avalanche of Media Leaks is Harming National Security.* In the 24-page majority staff report, the committee argued, "the unauthorized disclosure of certain information can cost American lives."

The report was written after several leaks about the Trump administration and its governing style. Although the report was lauded by many Republicans, Democrats were quick to judge it, saying the committee's report didn't mention any specific examples of actual harm the leaks had on national security.

Although there has certainly been a greater number of leaks during the Trump presidency compared to administrations past, anonymous leaks to the press have been around since the founding of the United States.

At 91 years old, former FBI deputy director William Mark Felt, Sr. broke his 30-year silence to confirm he was *"Deep Throat,"* the anonymous government source that leaked information about the Watergate scandal.

At the time, Felt gave two Washington Post journalists, Bob Woodward and Carl Bernstein, confidential information that would lead them to crack the Watergate story. As Woodward and Bernstein pressed the president for answers, he dismissed their claims calling it a, *"witch hunt."*

In more recent times, former President George W. Bush felt the pressure of several surveillance-related leaks. In 2005, the New York Times published an article about the so-called, "warrantless wiretapping program." Under the program, the National Security Administration could listen in on any Americans phone calls without a warrant. The wiretapping was legal under the Terrorist

Surveillance Program, which was set up in response to the 9/11 attacks.

President Barack Obama has also faced the annoyance of governmental leaks. During the Obama Administration, Army Pvt. Bradley, now Chelsea Manning, leaked hundreds of thousands of diplomatic cables and military reports to WikiLeaks. Similarly, NSA contractor Edward Snowden disclosed the details of the inner workings of highly classified U.S. programs.

Although irritation towards leaks is a universal feeling shared throughout every presidency, Nate Schenkaan, a project director at Freedom House - which advocates for democratic, political and human rights - argues leaks do not constitute a deep state.

Leaks

The influence of other public servants — specifically career military officers like John Kelly, James Mattis, and H.R. McMaster — has been referenced as symptomatic of the kind of influence any alleged deep state organization, no matter how loosely affiliated, could have on not just the Trump presidency, but in theory the policies of any sitting president. Seen by some in the media as an attempt to reign in what many felt to be reckless or ill-advised Trump policies, the supposed effect that secretive or covert actions by others in the Trump White House acting against the president they purportedly serve is also claimed by some to be evidence pointing to the existence of the so-called deep state.

An anonymous opinion-editorial piece famously published by the New York Times in September of 2018 seemed to offer perhaps a more nuanced view of what could be called the "*deep state phenomenon.*" The article, titled "I Am Part of the Resistance Inside the Trump Administration" was allegedly penned by a senior official in that administration and was deeply critical of Trump and his performance as president.

The anonymous author claimed to be one of *"many senior officials" working from inside the Trump Administration to curtail or stymy efforts by President Trump to enact legislation or policy by "working diligently from within to frustrate parts of his agenda and his worst inclinations."*

Though the identity — and actual influence or importance — of the anonymous author was called into question on the grounds that many different individuals could be considered "senior officials," many of Trump's supporters and other believers of the deep state theory saw this as a kind of vindication.

The other side of information equation

The deep state information ecosystem doesn't just focus on sharing government information to affect policies and election outcomes, it also continuously collects and monitors information recorded, saved and shared by its ordinary citizens. Now why would the deep state need that data? Simple. Knowledge = Power. The power to *"take the public's temperature."* The power to identify important trends in public opinion, possibly gauge whether the propaganda (if present) is working and gather intel from communities that may not be captured in reports

or on news websites. Having citizen's private information at their disposal gives the deep state the right opportunities to advance its agenda in an informed fashion.

How do they do it? The intelligence ecosystem. The deep state has access to the CIA, the NSA and the FBI.

A refresher on definitions

CIA — Central Intelligence Agency
NSA — National Security Agency
FBI — Federal Bureau of Investigation

Deep state, along with the government itself, is collecting data on you from all available sources – like your home and cell phones, emails, computers, tablets, Smart TVs, satellites, and more. You are being photographed from your computer camera and from satellite cameras, your conversations are being recorded and your texts and emails are being read.

Technology has become vital to our lives. Cell phones, smart watches, tracking watches with cell service for kids, tablets, laptops, drones, wi-fi cameras, smart home equipment and all the other tools that we feel we need to fully engage in today's life also come with a caveat – the built-in ability to spy on you. Anything that has wi-fi capability can technically be hacked.

The Surveillance Infrastructure is

Everywhere

Yes, every move you make is recorded, and by now, that shouldn't come as a surprise. Logging everything you do is a life's mission of social media companies, internet service providers, email services and search engines. Surveillance cameras are everywhere in public and embedded in devices you bring into your home. And those are just the private companies surveilling your life.

At the government level, the deep state's most notorious spies - the Central Intelligence Agency - use surveillance with a reach and sophistication that is genuinely frightening. But you can take steps to remain free and unmonitored.

Using Alexa, Cortana - or whatever cute name they choose - the companies behind the 'Internet of Things' continually eavesdrop on you and your family. Ironically, you have invited them in by purchasing their devices and paying for their services. This pervasive surveillance extends to cell phone microphones that are never off, TV voice-command that is never muted, and cars that automatically record your movements.

A cell phone is one of the easiest things to track and while government agencies are authorized to track anyone's cell phone with a warrant, they take the liberty to spy on you without a just cause. Knowing where your cell phone is located at any given moment reveals all of your private data – when you are hanging out with friends, when you are at a dentist appointment, when you are going out to eat, where you sleep on any given night. Coupled with your credit or debit card data and social media data, this information literally provides a pretty good picture of your life, activities, beliefs, relationships and spending habits. On top of it, government agencies snag your contact lists from your phones and emails, keep track of your call records and more. This goes far beyond simply scanning for keywords that may signal a national security issue. It's literally about keeping tabs on everything you do – in case this data is ever required for the deep state agenda.

So how do they track you exactly? The deep state's "machine" uses Stingrays – devices that act like fake cell phone towers to trick cell phones into releasing their locations. The police, the CIA, the NSA and other agencies have been using these snooping devices for years with little to no oversight. If you ask a member of the general public what a Stingray is – most will have no clue, because very few discovered cases of their use make it to public news sites.

Your Smart TV, Smart Fridge, security system and just about anything else with light and buttons uses cellular connection, wi-fi connection and Internet to transmit loads of information.

Even Your Car is Watching! One of the most sinister private partnerships in recent years is the installation of monitoring devices, including cameras and microphones, in new cars. Dealers say it is for your safety and protection, but insurance companies love them since they reveal so much about your driving habits.

Naturally, the deep state is interested in the location, driving routines and conversations of people it is watching.

The moral? The more aware you are, the better you can protect yourself – and well give you some tips on that in chapter 5.

CHAPTER 4:

A Culture of Conflict

Aside from leaks, one reason the concept of a deep state has thrived within the Trump Presidency is the deep division between political parties. According to a 2017 study by the Pew Research Center, the divisions between Republicans and Democrats on fundamental political values reached record levels during the Obama presidency. Yet, within the first year of Trump's political rein, the gap grew even larger.

Pew discovered deep divides on government, race, immigration, national security, and environmental protection. The study found party largely determines which side Americans stand on most issues, dividing people more than race, religion, education, or age.

As this culture of conflict becomes more deeply rooted in U.S. politics, Americans on both sides of the aisle feel more isolated from the other

Pew Research Center

side. According to a 2018 NBC/Wall Street Journal poll, 80% of Americans feel the country is *"mainly"* or *"totally"* divided.

The well-meaning deep state

This divide has even been felt within the Trump White House. In the aforementioned New York Times op-ed titled *"I Am Part of the Resistance Inside the Trump Administration,"* an anonymous senior white house official explains how they, and their colleagues, are fighting the president from within the administration.

This article, which lead the president to use the term "deep state," publicly for the first time, shook the nation with its refreshing candor and tantalizing anonymity.

The author states, *"many of the senior officials in [Trump's] own administration are working diligently from within to frustrate parts of his agenda and his worst inclinations. I would know. I am one of them."*

Although the author admits to being a part of an inside resistance, the author dismisses the claim of a deep state saying, *"To be clear, ours is not the popular 'resistance' of the left. We want the administration to succeed..."*

Although the author stated they wanted the administration to succeed, the president and his cabinet were quick to respond

with fury. The president's first reaction was a tweet that singularly read: "TREASON?"

Press Secretary Sarah Sanders also submitted a statement, saying, "the individual behind this piece has chosen to deceive, rather than support, the duly elected President of the United States... the coward should do the right thing and resign."

Deep state in the furniture business?

The conflict has only been growing and in some cases it's almost ridiculous. In a March 2018 article, Huffington Post discusses the use of the term *"deep state"* by Rep. Claudia Tenney in regard to Ben Carson's expensive dining set purchase. Huffington is quick

to say her deep state claim is unfounded. Apparently, Carson denied buying the dining set for his office and Tenney claimed that none of his staff bought it. The article then offers a transcript from a radio show wherev Tenney made the comment:

"Somebody in the deep state — it was not one of his people, apparently — ordered a table, like a conference room table or whatever it was, for a room," Tenney said. "And that's what the cost was. Ben Carson tried to — he said, "You know how hard it is to turn it back because of the way that the procurement

happens?"

Huffington, on the other hand, claims that Carson's wife purchased the table and Carson was fully aware.

HuffPost also ripped into Eric Trump for his #DeepState tweets and proposing that Ellen Degeneres is a part of deep state.

Disproving the deep state theory or serving the deep state agenda?

On August 8, 2019, The Washington Post published a memo by Chuck Park – a now former U.S. Foreign Service officer. In his letter, Park speaks about the reason for his resignation and refutes the deep state theories. He proposes that we call it "The Complacent State" instead. He writes:

"...almost three years since his election, what I have not seen is organized resistance from within. To the contrary, two senior Foreign Service officers admonished me for risking my career when I signed an internal dissent cable against the ban on travelers from several majority-Muslim countries in January 2017. Among my colleagues at the State Department, I have met neither the unsung hero nor the cunning villain of deep state lore. If the resistance does exist, it should be clear by this point that it has failed."

Whether he is right or is a pawn in the deep state's agenda is up to your own interpretation.

One thing is true – he is not alone, and many officials and civil servants have either quit or been replaced since Trump took office.

CHAPTER 5:

Taking Action

Whatever your personal opinion of the deep state theory, its proponents or its detractors, there are many who are convinced of its existence. In their view, the alleged deep state government functioning in the shadows of the legitimate and elected U.S. government is composed of a combination of politicians from both the legislative and executive branches, including high-ranking committee members, representatives of the military, and shadowy elites linked to the military-industrial complex, major banking institutions, and tech giants.

Though there is little proof of any cohesive organization that fits this description, the term (for better or worse) has entered the lexicon of American politics and is likely to be redefined and reapplied to various bodies or interest groups in the future. Whether real or not, the deep state — as a concept and political

shorthand—is here to stay.

Those who believe in its existence argue it lies within the vast belly of bureaucracy. The federal government has over 2 million employees, not including postal workers.

As part of Trump's campaign platform, he promised to "drain the swamp." This now iconic phrase alludes to eliminating many of those federal jobs, including positions within the white house. So far, President Trump has maintained that promise, with over half of the top jobs at the State Department still sitting vacant.

According to Evan Osnos, a staff writer for The New Yorker, "draining the swamp," has been Trump's main plan of attack on a deep state. He told Fresh Air, "Donald Trump would talk about the war on the deep state, by which he meant the power elite, the permanent bureaucracy, the people who were, in his vision, sort of running things behind the scene."

Since the "deep state" is synonymous with leaks against the White House, there is potential room for legal action. Former President Barack Obama was infamous for pressing charges against people who leaked sensitive information to the press.

Although the Trump administration has announced intentions to go after all leakers, only some instances of leaking is criminal in nature. Typically, classified leaks and stolen information can be prosecuted against. However, if a government agency is violating the law or abusing it's authority all leaks are considered legal under the Whistleblower Protection Act.

The Complex State

Although deep states have shown their true colors in other nations, such as Egypt and Turkey, the belief in a U.S. based deep state still rides deeply on party lines. While the political divide within the nation certainly leads to some politicians to undermine the president, liberals argue a complex, succinct resistance designed to overthrow the president does not exist. In contrast, conservatives are quick to protect the president, saying any attack on his rhetoric is an attack on our nation.

Protect yourself against deep state spying

The less deep state knows about you, the less control they will have over you. Being anonymous in this day and age is hard, but it is worth it. Here are some expert tips on how to do just that.

Do not use cloud storage providers

The reason Google, Gmail, OneDrive, Hotmail, Facebook, or WhatsApp are Free is because they are happy to store and sell your information. The deep state is all to eager to use this data to learn everything they can about you.

Avoid public WIFI

Anybody can access public WIFI and there are lots of criminals who can easily steal your data from there – passwords included. Deep state is one of them.

Be aware

By now you understand just how much you are being watched. Most of everything you do is tracked and the information is accessible to the Government, the deep state and the criminals who manage to hack into the same surveillance tools.

You can defeat this frightening trampling of your privacy by holding sensitive, private conversations outside the presence of electronic devices. Leave your cell phones in one room and move to a closet, storeroom, or patio where you can speak out of reach of surveillance gear. Speaking in low tones also frustrates Deep state spies, since separating soft voices from ambient hiss is very difficult.

Unplug

Cell phone networks and your internet connection, including Wi-Fi, transmit private moments stolen by the electronics in your home to the CIA. When your computers are not in use, unplug your router or cable connection. Yes, this is an inconvenience - you will have to wait for the computer to reconnect when you need it. But doing so prevents transmission of data.
Make it a habit, and you will be glad you did.

Deny Power to Your Devices

The 'off' and 'sleep' modes on your TV and other devices may lull you into believing they are offline when they are not. They are powered and capable of recording you merely by being plugged in. How to foil this sinister built-in surveillance feature? Unplug it! The effect is akin to throwing water on the Wicked Witch of the West.

No electric power, no surveillance power!

Bag Your Phone

Your cell phone is active even when it is switched off. Most phones no longer have detachable batteries, giving you no options for cutting power.

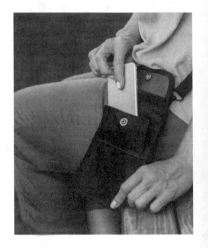

The best way to prevent deep state actors from using cell networks to access your communications is to place your phone in an RF-proof shielding bag. Ironically, deep state actors use them all the time to prevent access to cell phones seized as evidence.

You can use them, too. Shield bags are readily available and a simple way to protect your wireless devices from outside interference.

Be Selective in Your Record Keeping

Search warrants – whether justified or not – routinely uncover self-incriminating evidence in the form of notes, plans, journals and drawings. You can deprive the deep state from seizing your private records by keeping as few as possible. Consider committing to memory anything you may be tempted write down or share the information verbally (in a secure location) with a trusted friend or family member. The more you reduce your paper trial, the better.

Privacy over fashion

Remember, your car is watching you. Naturally, the deep state is interested in the location, driving routines and conversations of people it is watching, so don't make it easy for them. Cars ten years or older are free of these surveillance devices, and while they are still on the road and reliable, consider augmenting your privacy by driving one.

Your Cell Phone: deep state's BFF

As we explained in Chapter 3, your cell phone is not private at all. The news media has discovered the Stingray, a portable device that intercepts nearby cell phone signals by mimicking a cell tower. Authorities claim most reported instances of  Stingray intercepts are the work of foreign spies, but the evidence suggests otherwise.

The potential for deep state abuse is obvious since Stingray enables live eavesdropping and real-time phone tracking.

Even before Stingray, your cell phone was and still is a goldmine of personal information for electronically savvy deep state operatives. It tracks your texts, your location, your browsing history, your phone calls, your photographs, your social media, and, depending on the apps you download, your emails and your music choices.

All this information is available to the deep state with a few keystrokes. It's the perfect surveillance device since everyone has one, usually on their person. From the deep state perspective, you are wearing a self-installed 'wire.'

You can take steps to ward them off, however.

• Reduce surveillance opportunities and wean yourself from 'device addiction' by only taking your phone with you when it's necessary. Practice leaving it at home. You will be surprised at how easy it is to forget all about it for a few hours, and you frustrate the watchers.

• Assume all your cellular activity is either being actively monitored or recorded in deep state databases. Be selective about the content of your texts, what you photograph, and your internet browsing.

• Get accustomed to turning off your phone when not in use and placing it in the RF-proof shield bag mentioned above.

• Review your downloaded apps and eliminate as many as possible. Apps collect user information that is easily accessible to CIA electronic snooping. Be selective about which apps you download in the future.

48

Encrypt everything

Despite having access to the best technology, the deep state would still take a long time to break an encryption algorithm. Be sure to encrypt your emails and your hard drive.

Keep your mail [more] private

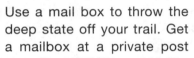

Use a mail box to throw the deep state off your trail. Get a mailbox at a private post store like UPS Store of Mailboxes Etc. They keep your information on record only within that particular store so it's a lot harder to get to.

Wake up and be present

Aside from protecting your privacy, the key action you can take against the deep state is being present. What we mean by that is that you should participate in our democracy. Being present when and where decisions are made means that you are not only in the loop but you have a say, and an opportunity to challenge the deep state.

Vote in the Presidential election

Sure, maybe your vote doesn't shut down the deep state's agenda, but it certainly makes a difference in who we as a country put in the office. Plus, if your name is on a ballot, it's harder for someone else to put it on one – if you know what we mean…

Vote in state and local elections

These votes are very important as it's these people on a state and local level who end up having a lot of pull as far as local policy changes. Local policy changes set precedents for policy changes on a state and national level. Don't ignore these "small" elections. They count! Get to know your candidates, their interests, agendas and connections – and make your voice heard.

Participate in your local government

Take the local vote a step further. Run for a local official position, participate in the city hall, attend hearing meetings. Important decisions are made every day and they can be made with your participation and awareness or without. Is something important to you? Start a petition or sign an existing one, rally your neighborhood to deal with a problem, write letters to your representatives or campaign for a candidate you believe in.

Take a stand

You don't have to participate in protests to take a stand. One great option is to take up community journalism. You have access to number of platforms where you can effectively communicate your message and reach people. We live in a global, connected world and reporting, sharing opinion or challenging big media outlets has become easier than ever.

While the extent of the deep state in the US is unknown and much of what we read about is speculation, corruption exists within any and every government. People and organizations exist

to serve their own interests and it's no secret that donations and friendships have long determined certain decisions within our local, state and national government.

The more concerned citizens like you and I participate in the government, take part in the discussion, uncover and report the truth and challenge possible fake news, the more aware the general public will be and the fewer opportunities the deep state players will have to influence elected officials, sway policies and quietly push their agenda. Simply being an agent for accountability can be enough to thwart the deep state – whatever form it may be taking.

CHAPTER 6:

Resources

How The Deep State Came To America: A History
https://warontherocks.com/2019/02/how-the-deep-state-came-to-america-a-history/

Don't Fear the Deep State. It's the Shallow State That Will Destroy Us.
https://foreignpolicy.com/2019/02/04/dont-fear-the-deep-state-its-the-shallow-state-that-will-destroy-us-trump-theresa-may-netanyahu-brexit-israel-populism/

Does Trump Have the Balls to Hold the Deep State Accountable?
https://www.foreignpolicyjournal.com/2019/07/10/does-trump-have-the-balls-to-hold-the-deep-state-accountable/

The Deep State Digs Deeper
https://spectator.org/the-deep-state-digs-deeper/

The Overstock CEO Resigned Claiming 'Deep State' Conspiracy and a Relationship With a Russian Spy. Here's What to Know
https://time.com/5659811/overstock-ceo-russian-spy-conspiracy-theory/

Putin suggests US 'deep state' working against Trump
https://thehill.com/policy/international/430877-putin-suggests-us-deep-state-working-against-trump

The Deep State Is Real. But it might not be what you think.
https://www.politico.com/magazine/story/2017/09/05/deep-state-real-cia-fbi-intelligence-215537

President Trump's Allies Keep Talking About the 'Deep State.' What's That?
https://time.com/4692178/donald-trump-deep-state-breitbart-barack-obama/

Here's the Memo That Blew Up the NSC. Fired White House staffer argued "deep state" attacked Trump administration because the president represents a threat to cultural Marxist memes, globalists, and bankers.
https://foreignpolicy.com/2017/08/10/heres-the-memo-that-blew-up-the-nsc/

State Secrets: How An Avalanche Of Media Leaks Is Harming National Security
https://www.hsgac.senate.gov/imo/media/doc/2017-07-06 State Secrets report.pdf

US Senate report on leaks and national security is deeply flawed
https://cpj.org/blog/2017/07/us-senate-report-on-leaks-and-national-security-is-1.php

How 'Deep Throat' Took Down Nixon From Inside the FBI

https://www.history.com/news/watergate-deep-throat-fbi-informant-nixon

Lawmakers Grapple With Warrantless Wiretapping Program
https://thehill.com/policy/national-security/351272-lawmakers-grapple-with-warrantless-wiretapping-program

The NSA Program To Detect And Prevent Terrorist Attacks Myth V. Reality
https://www.justice.gov/archive/opa/docs/nsa_myth_v_reality.pdf

Trump Joins Long History Of Presidents Fuming Over Leaks
https://www.politico.com/story/2017/08/03/trump-presidents-vent-over-leaks-241306

I Am Part of the Resistance Inside the Trump Administration
https://www.nytimes.com/2018/09/05/opinion/trump-white-house-anonymous-resistance.html

Political Polarization In The American Public
http://www.people-press.org/2014/06/12/section-1-growing-ideological-consistency/

The Partisan Divide on Political Values Grows Even Wider
http://www.people-press.org/2017/10/05/the-partisan-divide-on-political-values-grows-even-wider/

As partisan divides over political values widen, other gaps remain more modest
http://www.people-press.org/2017/10/05/the-partisan-divide-on-political-values-grows-even-wider/takeaways_fix1/

Twitter -- Real Donald Trump
https://twitter.com/realDonaldTrump/status/1037464177269514240

Twitter -- White House Press Secretary
https://tinyurl.com/y34tey3f

Dissent Memo Circulating In The State Department Over Trump's Policy On Refugees And Immigrants
https://www.washingtonpost.com/world/national-security/dissent-memo-circulating-in-the-state-department-over-trumps-policy-on-refugees-and-immigrants/2017/01/30/c1457689-5108-4ef7-bcea-1a5dee431ef8_story.html

How Trump Can Strike Back at the Deep State
https://www.theatlantic.com/ideas/archive/2018/09/its-not-just-the-deep-state-trump-should-worry-about/569995/

Federal Employees By State
http://www.governing.com/gov-data/federal-employees-workforce-numbers-by-state.html

What's With All Trump's Talk About "Draining the Swamp"?
https://slate.com/human-interest/2016/10/why-do-trump-and-his-supports-keep-talking-about-draining-the-swamp.html

Trump rages about leakers. Obama quietly prosecuted them.
https://www.washingtonpost.com/news/the-fix/wp/2017/06/08/trump-rages-about-leakers-obama-quietly-prosecuted-them/

Leaks And The Media
https://www.freedomforuminstitute.org/first-amendment-center/primers/leaks-and-the-media/

Sean Hannity: The Deep State And The Greatest Abuse Of Power, Corruption In American History
https://www.foxnews.com/opinion/sean-hannity-the-deep-*state-and-the-greatest-abuse-of-power-corruption-in-american-history*